# The Ultimate Big Crazy Wifi Antenna Guide

Projects, tips, and mods for

longer range wifi.

**Philip G Collier**

# DEDICATION

To all of the people out there in the world who find themselves in a crowd of people asking, "why," and ask, "why not," then take action to improve things where they are. To all of the people who said, "I'm going to fix this - not just for myself, but for us all."

# Table of Contents

# DISCLAIMER

This book covers the topic of wireless networking antennas, device modification, and high power wifi operation, for entertainment and educational purposes. Follow the applicable wireless and computing laws and regulations of your country and jurisdiction. Modify, build, and operate wireless equipment at your own risk. Information in this book is presented without any warranties or guarantees as to suitability for any purpose.

# Overview: Long Haul Wifi FTW

Wifi antenna projects shown here will offer advantages if you want to make long wifi links between your device and an access point, or between two devices. They improve reception of distant signals and focus more of your transmitted signal on distant points. Your internet connection runs at top speed when signals are strong.

Give favor to the antennas based on parabolic reflectors. As I write these words in 2022, we are well into the age of advanced wifi and 5G mobile service, and you can enjoy plentiful antenna gain on those services by mounting a wireless adapter or data dongle at the focus of the parabola. Wifi 5, 6, and 7 use multiple frequency bands, so it is not practical to build unique feeders for each band. From the dongle, run a USB cable to a nearby computer to enjoy internet access.

An even better way to share internet from a parabolic antenna is not to run USB cable to a computer several meters away, but to attach the dongle to a small Raspberry Pi or Beaglebone mounted at the antenna. Within the 'Pi or 'Bone, configure the networking software to run a *bridge* between the wifi device and its internal ethernet. Then run ethernet cable out of the 'Pi or 'Bone to a separate router or computer. Such a lash up can supply internet to an office or home.

In the chapters to follow, the book dives into a mix of calculation and construction of antennas using fairly short wavelengths. Neither is very difficult, but it is certainly easier if you can measure, cut, and solder sheet metal and wire down to millimeter accuracy. The calculations are included to show a more complete process and to open the door for you to try variations and experiment. If you have been doing antenna calculations on a handheld device, put it down and get familiar with the great tools which can do calculations on your PC. Make friends with the shell environment, Python, and Java. I found the doors of a whole new world opening wide upon doing that; so can you!

Think of this as a workbook as much as an instructional text or handbook. Ample space is provided on the pages for your handwritten notes or annotations.

Wireless is evolving quickly. We are moving from an environment where long haul connections could make a big difference in connectivity for people on the fringe to one where bandwidth matters more. Bandwidth is mattering more each day, while there are more and more Wifi 5, 6, and 5G access points, with wifi 7 at the gate.

What I find exciting about wireless networking trends is movement toward the mesh: a robust wifi infrastructure built upon plentiful devices not very far apart. Thus, big antennas are going to be less important for most people. However, many of you will need some gain and power to connect from points "not in the middle of the action."

None of this is surprising. In fact, that is how the frontier moves. Enjoy the frontier before it is gone; enjoy the thick bandwidth of next gen wireless when it finally moves in around you.

# A Linear Focus Parabolic Antenna

Parabolic wifi antennas are generally thought of as dish shaped objects – a three dimensional curved reflector with a yagi, biquad, or helical radiator at the focal point, aimed into the dish. An alternative is the two dimensional "linear focus" reflector. It is a two dimensional expression of a parabola, which focuses energy along a "focal line" instead of one point. It works quite well with simple dipole antennas.

Design of a linear focus antenna is as simple as selecting a suitable parabolic curve, plotting it as a template on a flat surface, and fitting sheet metal or wire mesh to fit the parabola.

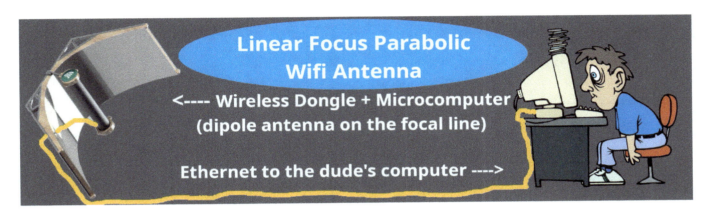

Doing the parabolic wifi antenna design calculations by hand is time consuming; there is plenty of excellent and free software you can use to create a template in minutes. An easy way to calculate and plot a good curve is to use a script written in the Python language. Python is great, as it is a simple matter to install in Windows, Linux, Mac OS, or any of the BSD operating systems.

See Appendix I for the code listing of a parabola calculator script, which I run in Linux with a simple shell terminal command:

```
python3 ./parabola.py
```

To create a usable template, scale the image in an editor, setting it to 300 pixels per inch (118 pixels per cm). The squares are 1 cm on a side. Print the image, maintaining 300 pixels per inch. Use enough paper to print the whole template.

The most important thing is that the image scaling is linear, preserving the ratio of length vs width, and scale such that a measurement of 10 cm on the x axis equals 10 cm on the y axis. Many texts on design and building of parabolic reflector antennas assert that the f/D ratio (focal length /diameter) should be between 0.3 and 0.6 for optimal performance. Low f/D radio reflectors work better with less directive feeds, such as a simple dipole. High f/D reflectors work well with more directive feeds, such as a two element yagi. The linear focus design is less limiting, as the toroidally shaped antenna pattern works fine in a deep, low f/D antenna such as this.

This linear focus parabolic wifi antenna physically consists of a sheet of metal shaped to precisely fit a two dimensional parabolic curve. It can be built in a couple of hours and involves a fair amount of measuring, cutting, bending, and bolting of metal. Put it up and enjoy a very durable antenna that provides great signals.

Gain is about 15 dB over a dipole, and depends greatly on the quality of construction. Of greatest importance is shaping the sheet metal to accurately follow the parabolic curve given in the template. Parts may be found at large hardware retailers such as "Home Depot" or local scrap metal dealers. Versions of this antenna have been made using automotive sheet metal; others use wire mesh. Use whatever material you must, but make sure to follow the curve.

As with parabolic dishes, it is critically important that the feeder antenna be precisely mounted at the focus. Make note of the focus as given in the template and construct the mount carefully so that the wifi dipole is centered on that focal line. If using a two or three element wifi yagi feeder, set the driven element along the focal line.

Notes: _____

_____

_____

_____

_____

Linear Focus Parabolic Antenna Template

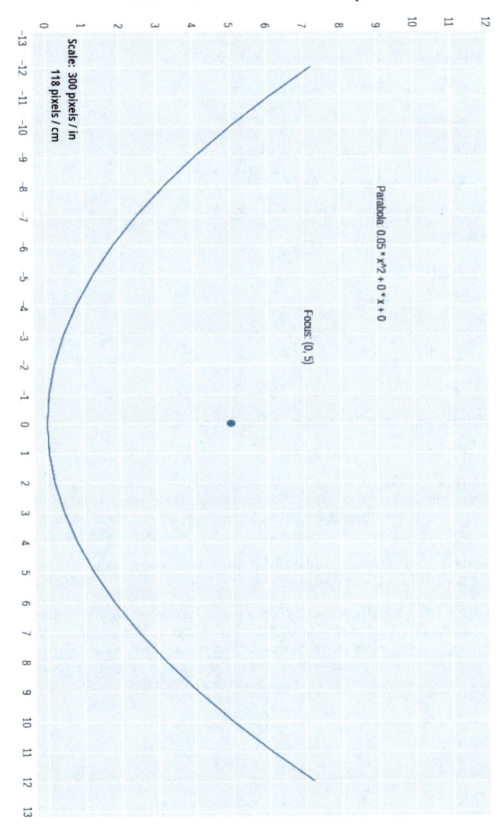

Scale: 300 pixels / in
118 pixels / cm

Parabola: 0.05 * x^2 + 0 * x + 0

Focus: (0, 5)

## Parts & Equipment List:

1.  one 36" x 2" aluminum flat (to be referenced as flat "A")

2.  one 36" x 1" aluminum flat (to be referenced as flat "B")

3.  one 14" x 36" sheet of aluminum flashing

4.  metal cutting shears

5.  a yardstick or tape measure

6.  three 6-32 x 3/4 machine screws (the long screws)

7.  two 6-32 x 3/8 machine screws (the short screws)

8.  five 6-32 machine screw nuts

9.  one drill with a 1/8" bit

10. one fine point felt tip marker

11. two clamps

12. a pair of pliers

13. a hacksaw

14. Parabolic Template, printed as a poster, carefully aligned and taped

To get started with the measuring, bending, drilling, and cutting, lay down the template and the assortment of parts. You will measure and mark the parts first, then do the metal work. If it is necessary to erase and redo any marks on the metal, scrubbing the metal with a moistened paper towel or rag works well. I usually apply a bit of alcohol to the rag to make it more effective, but soapy water is okay for the cleaning.

It is extremely helpful to have clamps available to hold the parts stationary while cutting. A drill press is not a hard requirement, but it is a good thing to have for drilling clean, straight holes in the flats.

Although the list above calls for machine screws, I have built a version of the linear focus antenna using pop rivets. They work. Screws and pop rivets can both loosen over time, producing a somewhat "clanky and clopitty" antenna which makes noise when moved or subject to vibration. Perhaps washers and nylon grommets could help make for a quieter, tighter antenna after a year or two; precise work on the initial construction results in a longer time before the aged frame gets its first bit of rattle.

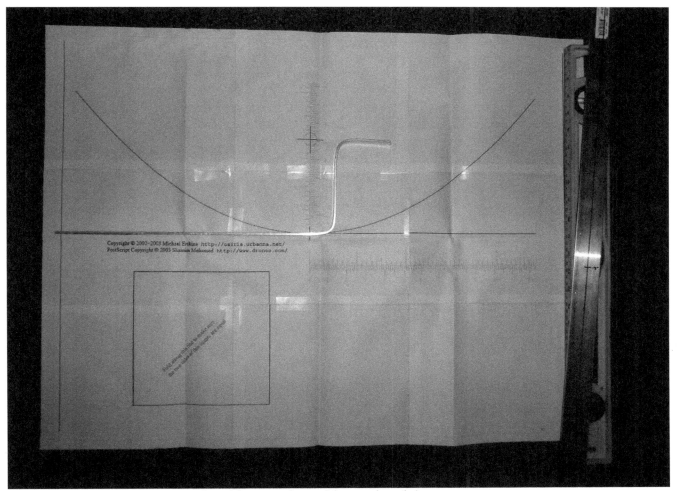

An older template with metalwork in progress.

## Assembly Procedure:

1. Mark all flats and flashing from edge to edge along their center lines and across midpoints, both sides.

2. Mark dots on flat "A" along its center line, one inch in from the ends and at the center. For a 36" length of metal, the marks will go on at 1, 18, and 35 inches.

3. Carefully drill holes through the marked points.

4. Abeam the hole at the middle of flat "A" drill holes on both sides, 1/2" inside of the edges. This results in a row of 3 across the flat at the 18" point. This is the center line, where the flat "B" will be attached.

5. Set flat "A" along its edge, and bend it to fit the parabolic template. Bend a

little at a time, working along the length of the metal.

6.  Mark flat "B" across the 15" point, beyond there by a distance equal to the focal distance on the template, and finally 3" beyond the focal distance mark.

7.  Bend flat "B" to a 90 degree angle at the 15" line. Bend flat "B" 90 degrees in the opposite direction at the second mark (representing the focal distance). Flat "B" should now have a right angled "Z" shape.

8.  Use the hacksaw to cut flat "B" at the third mark.

9.  Mark across flat "B" at 7 1/2" from its long end (halfway to its first bend)

10.  Clamp flat "A" onto the outside of flat "B" such that the three holes in the middle of "A" are on the center line of "B" AND the middle hole in "A" is on the 7 1/2" mark on "B"

11.  Make sure "A" and "B" are perfectly perpendicular and positioned as     specified above, then drill through the existing holes an and into "B." "B"   will then have three holes through its center line that match the holes  across "A."

Checking fit of bolts / 3 holes before attaching metal flashing.

12. Clamp the flashing onto "A" along the inside of the curve, carefully along the center lines, and drill through the existing holes near the ends of "A," making holes in the flashing. Insert the short screws through the flashing and "A." Apply nuts and finger tighten for a fit check, then remove the nuts.

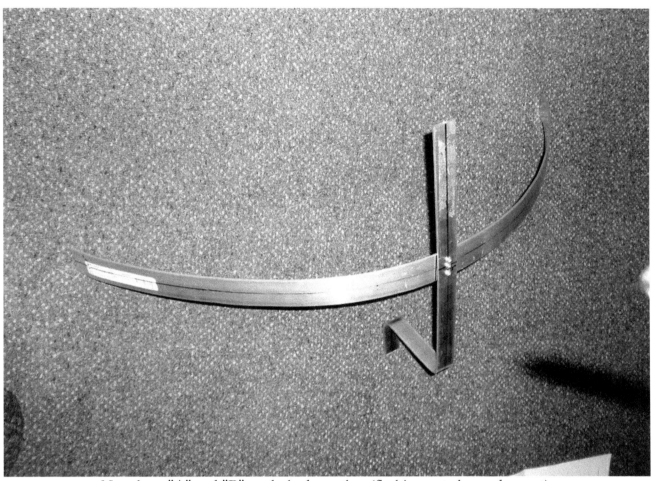

Note how "A" and "B" are bolted together (flashing not clamped on yet).

13. Place flat "B" against the back of flat "A," with the Z bend extending under reflector and toward focal line. Line up the 3 holes and push the long screws through the flashing, "A," and "B." Apply nuts and tighten securely.

After tightening the nuts on the back of flat "B," most of the reflector is complete.

Rear view of the linear focus reflector. Attach electronics to the bottom of flat "B."

If mounting the antenna outdoors, it will need an adjustable clamp or bracket to hold it rigidly in place. The dongle (and host SBC, if using a 'Pi or 'Bone ) should be set in a weather resistant housing and attached to flat "B" near the line of focus.

The antenna actually needs to be a few inches above the bottom of the reflector, on the line of focus, and approximately as high as the three bolts. It is a good idea to construct a short boom to hold the electronics above flat "B" if not using an attachable dipole or collinear type of antenna.

Mount the assembled reflector and adapter in a window, on a balcony, or wherever there is a line of sight path to the desired wifi access point.

# A High Gain Prime Focus Dish Antenna

Presented here is a project showing how to convert common satellite TV antennas into high performance wifi dish antennas. A large 2 or 3 meter diameter wifi dish can provide 802.11 connections to access points dozens of kilometers away. Be aware that such long distance connections are possible only when the path is not obstructed by foliage, trees, or terrain. The best situation is to connect from hilltop to hilltop, or for city dwellers, between the tops of high rise buildings.

When used with a high power wifi adapter this kind of antenna is fantastic. Satellite dishes are easy to convert into wifi dish antennas. The essential change is replacing the satellite TV feedhorn with a mount to hold a classic wifi antenna. Wifi6 or wifi7 is available on all frequencies if a compatible dongle is mounted at the focal point. None of the manual "curve making" of scratch built parabolic reflectors is necessary. To successfully convert a dish for wifi use, you need a C or Ku band reflector in good condition and basic tools for measuring, cutting, and bolting parts.

Note that if your goal is to bring in wireless internet from another location and use it indoors, you should instead consider using a wireless bridge. If you want to provide strong wireless internet coverage to an outdoor area, but cannot provide a fiber optic or ethernet cable to your wireless router, again consider using a wireless bridge to substitute for the unavailable cable, and connect the bridge to a wifi router. The wifi router would then be available for all of the laptops, phones, or IOT devices in the area of interest. This is a better solution for situations such as these:

- Providing internet connectivity from one building to users in a remote house or office.

- Providing internet connectivity from one highrise building to another across town.

- Providing internet connectivity from an onshore location to users on an island or stationary boat.

- Sharing connectivity between two locations which can't be linked by cable.

Obtain an undamaged parabolic reflector designed for C or Ku band satellite television service. These are now inexpensive and abundant. The wifi dish pictured in this section was built from satellite TV gear junked by a local resident. Similar reflectors can be found in thrift stores, flea markets, and other habitats of electronics scroungers. Favor moderate to large Ku band reflectors (at least 76 cm or 30 inches diameter), since these will provide greater gain and directivity. Again, make sure the reflector is in good condition – not warped and free of dents! If it is merely rusty, that is okay. Use sandpaper to remove the rust, then repaint the reflector.

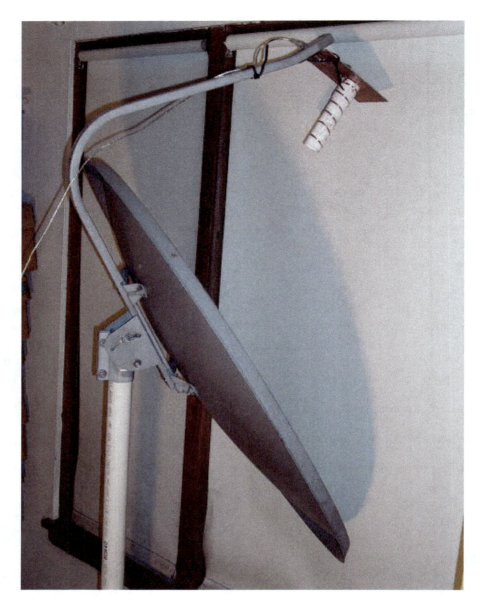

Satellite dish converted for long-range wifi.

## Building a Feed for the Wifi Dish Antenna

For very long range wireless networking, I have used a short 5 turn helical antenna, left hand polarized, with an 80 cm parabolic reflector. Signals were about 26 dB stronger than on a simple dipole! Mounting the helical wifi antenna was a matter of installing an angle bracket and bolting the helical wifi antenna into place at the dish focal point. It was necessary to slightly bend the bracket to aim the helix directly into the dish. A classic wifi dongle was mounted on the other side of the copper clad board, coupled to the helical antenna.

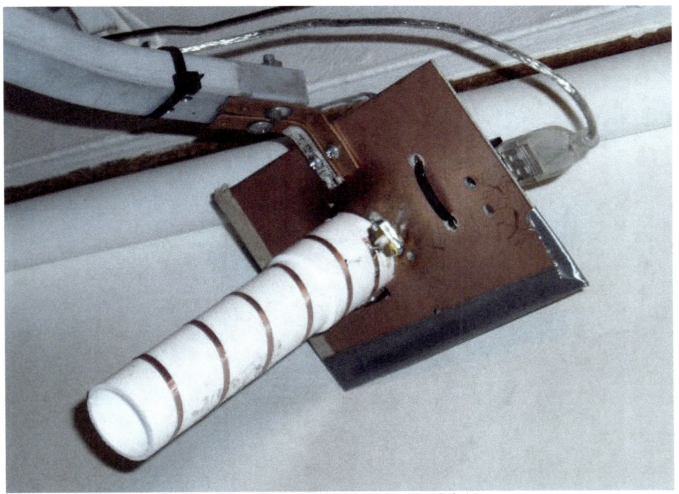

Short wifi helix feeding a parabolic wifi dish.

Another classic wifi dish antenna feeder option is a 3 or 4 element yagi mounted at the focal point and aimed into the reflector. I do not recommend any type of one-band antenna for Wifi6 or Wifi7 dongles. They work on multiple bands, so mount those with the antenna as close as possible to the exact focal point of the dish. Plan to connect the dongle to a Raspberry Pi or Beaglebone type of Single Board Computer (SBC). Bridge the ethernet and wifi so you can use an ethernet cable for connectivity to a wifi router or directly to your regular computer.

Note that a wifi biquad, or "cantenna" waveguide feed would work well in a wifi dish antenna, and would have a slight polarization advantage over a helical. Linearly polarized antennas have a slight advantage over helicals of the same size, but helicals perform better in rain or when there are many signal reflections.

The biquad wifi antenna pictured below was built out of junk parts one afternoon, and enabled very good long range 802.11 connections on its own. Mounted at the focal point of a surplus DirecTV dish, it provided full-scale signals from otherwise weak access points.

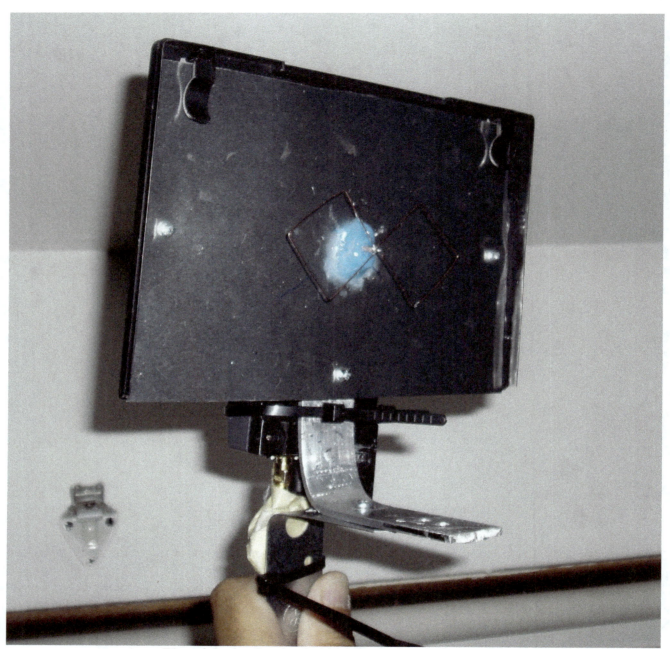

Biquad feeder for classic 802.11g, used with dish antenna.

## Mounting and Aiming the Wifi Dish Antenna

Installing a wifi dish antenna is more complex than it initially seems. Give thought to how it will be used: for a fixed point-to-point link, scanning the area for usable free hotspots, or as a portable link back to one's home access point? A fixed antenna can be aimed and bolted into place. A steerable or portable dish needs a means of securely mounting and aiming (motorized or by hand).

Offset feed antennas are popular, most originally designed for Ku band digital TV.

They require a special mounting and aiming technique. The best method is to invert the mounting hardware and angle the dish to about 75 degrees for peaking signals on the horizon. In azimuth, aim directly at the desired access point, but in elevation, offset about 37 degrees from dead center. My best of these, which stood for over a year, stood atop a vertical section of 2" schedule 40 pipe. A prime focus wifi dish, on the other hand, can simply be mounted on a pipe and aimed directly at the signal source.

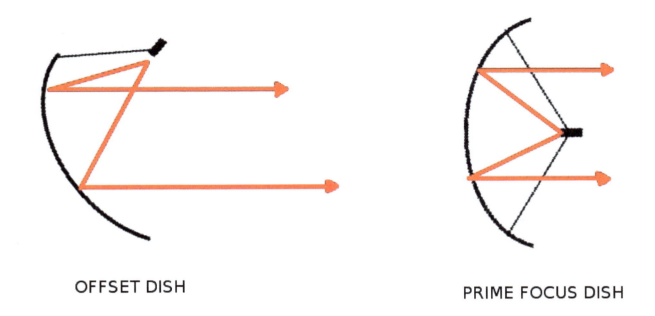

OFFSET DISH                    PRIME FOCUS DISH

Offset dishes require a different mounting technique when used for terrestrial wireless links. In most cases, simply inverting the mount enables easy aiming to the horizon. Typical offsets are 22 to 35 degrees. Therefore, set the dish to a 44 to 70 degree elevation angle for a horizontal beam. Prime focus dishes should be aimed directly at the source 0 degree elevation = horizontal beam.

Offset versus prime focus wifi dish antenna aiming.

Wifi dish antennas are very directional! It is common to scan an area and see weak signals just barely detectable when out of the beam. As the antenna is aimed directly at the distant access point, the signal strength will jump up considerably - perhaps to full scale. High directivity associated with wifi dish antennas is good: interference from off center stations is reduced and faster broadband connectivity is possible for distant access points.

All of the feed types for parabolic wifi antennas discussed here are intended for connection to USB wireless adapters. You should expect the best performance by using a wireless adapter equipped with a removable external antenna. Then, unscrew the original and replace it with the yagi, helical, or biquad homebuilt antennas. For Wifi6 or Wifi7 devices, continue to use the original antenna. Mount this at the reflector focal point and go for those connections across your farm, neighborhood, or town.

As to getting the wifi data into the computer, I'll repeat: use USB extension cables for short and simple runs. For a more permanent and useful distribution of broadband internet, connect the dongle to a single board computer, configuring a bridge between the wifi adapter and ethernet. Then run ethernet to your computer or a router which serves your home or office.

There have been some pretty interesting academic experiments with super long distance wifi. With dish diameters as high as 3 meters on both ends, experimenters established connections well over 100 km. The record holder at this time is Ermanno Pietrosemoli, who established a mountaintop to mountaintop link in the Andes of 238 km. Pietrosemoli used specialized Intel hardware, not common off the shelf equipment.

In most situations, you will not need any special networking settings to connect over a few kilometers. Plan to adjust your networking MTU and ACK timeout for connections beyond a few km. The defaults provide good broadband throughput; settings more favorable to distant connections reduce throughput on nearby access points. So, in summary: go with defaults for your specific hardware. Seek other MTU and ACK timeout numbers only if needed for connecting beyond several km.

# A High Gain Helical Antenna

Here is more detailed information on my unique helical wifi antenna, which may greatly extend your wireless networking range and speed. When built with ten or more turns, this 2.4 GHz wifi booster antenna vastly outperforms the cantennas and wi fi wok tops often seen on the internet. A short five turn helical makes a very good feeder for a wifi parabolic dish. A special quality of this antenna is that it radiates and receives a circularly polarized signal. It does not favor vertically or horizontally polarized signals. Thus, this antenna works well with wifi signals reflecting off of buildings, moving vehicles, or antennas oriented at odd angles. Circularly polarized signals are less affected by rain, so you can reach distant access points in stormy weather. There is a 3 dB loss of gain when using this antenna with linearly polarized signals; high gain is maintained by making the antenna long - at least ten turns for stand-alone usage.

## Parts required for the helical wifi antenna:

1. one square piece of copper sheet metal or single sided PC board for a ground plane.

2. one PVC kitchen drain tailpiece (3.8 cm / 1.5" diameter) to hold the helical windings

3. six 1/8" plastic cable ties

4. a length of copper circuit tape (adhesive backed, width 3mm or 1/8") or #14 copper wire

5. one suitable chassis connector (I used a reverse sma type matching the connector on my adapter)

6. one 90 degree angle bracket with screws and bolts to fit

## Construction:

1. Center the tailpiece on the PC board, copper side, and mark the circumference in ink.

2. Mark four locations on the circumference, spaced 90 degrees, where the cable ties will hold down the PVC tube.

3. Mark one location on the circumference, exactly between two 90 degree markings, where the coaxial connector will be mounted.

THIS DRAWING NOT TO SCALE:

Use for general guidance in marking
and drilling.

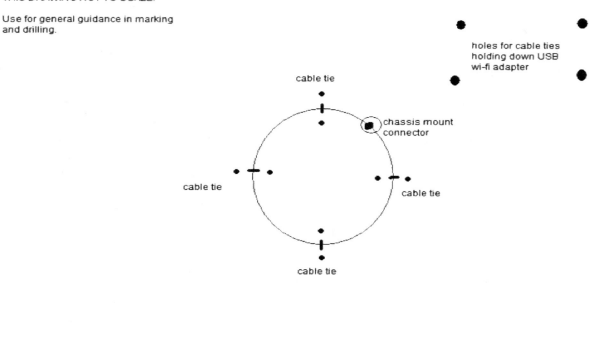

holes for cable ties
holding down USB
wi-fi adapter

cable tie

chassis mount
connector

cable tie

cable tie

cable tie

holes for right angle
bracket

AB9IL

A properly marked and drilled board for the helical wifi antenna.

1. Drill 1/8" holes on the inside and outside of the circumference at the cable tie locations.

2. Drill a hole directly on the circumference suitable for the chassis connector. Carefully measure and drill other holes for this connector if necessary.

3. Drill four holes, spaced 90 deg apart near the bottom end of the PVC tailpiece.

4. Drill holes to accommodate a small 90 degree corner bracket.

5. Drill holes on opposite side of board to accommodate USB wifi adapter that will be affixed with cable ties.

6. Tin the copper around the connector mounting hole, then mount the connector. Clip the center pin to keep it only long enough for connection to the helix windings.

7. Cut out a notch to accommodate the connector; it should clear center conductor, but avoid cutting out excess PVC material.

8. Feed cable ties through from the back side of the board, through holes in the tube, and back through the board. Tighten the cable ties, making sure the tube is firmly held to the copper ground plane.

9. Use a ruler and the edge of a sheet of paper to create a template for positioning the windings on the PVC tube. Distance zero represents the ground plane, then add the feedpoint distance, then ticks matching the turns spacing. Use the template to mark your tube on both the feedpoint side and the opposite side.

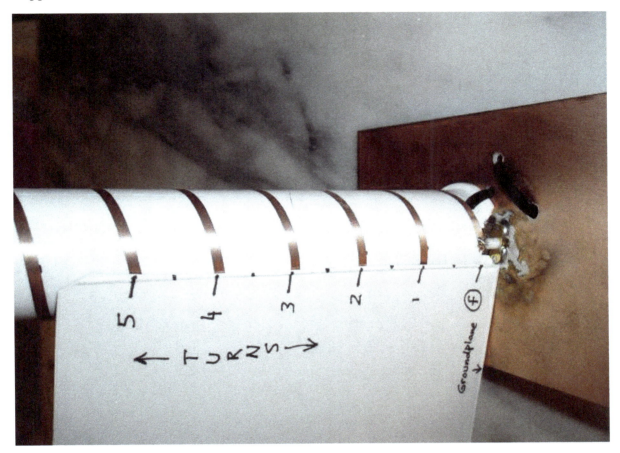

Space the turns 2.5 cm on a tube of 3.9 cm outer diameter.

Here is a table used for my prototype helical wifi antenna and its connector. Note that turn 1 starts at 0.8 cm (height above the ground plane). Turns Spacing is 2.5 cm, and the diameter is 3.9 cm (close enough for a 1.5" PVC tailpiece). If your connector can be trimmed to allow a feed connection closer to the ground plane than 0.8 cm, then simply run the helix as low as necessary. It is essential to keep the proper spacing between turns.

# Helical antenna turns data; start of turn and midway to next turn.

Spacing=2.5cm
Diameter=3.9cm
(fits 1.5" PVC tailpiece)

| Turn # | Height (cm) above groundplane | Half Turns Height (cm) |
|---|---|---|
| 1 (feedpoint) | 0.8 | 2.05 |
| 2 | 3.3 | 4.55 |
| 3 | 5.8 | 7.05 |
| 4 | 8.3 | 9.55 |
| 5 | 10.8 | 12.05 |
| 6 | 13.3 | 14.55 |
| 7 | 15.8 | 17.05 |
| 8 | 18.3 | 19.55 |
| 9 | 20.8 | 22.05 |
| 10 | 23.3 | 24.55 |
| 11 | 25.8 | 27.05 |
| 12 | 28.3 | 29.55 |
| 13 | 30.8 | 32.05 |

1. Carefully wind the helix, using circuit tape or wire, then solder to center conductor of chassis connector. Double check against the turns template. Polarization will be right-handed if the turns spiral clockwise (looking outward from the feedpoint).

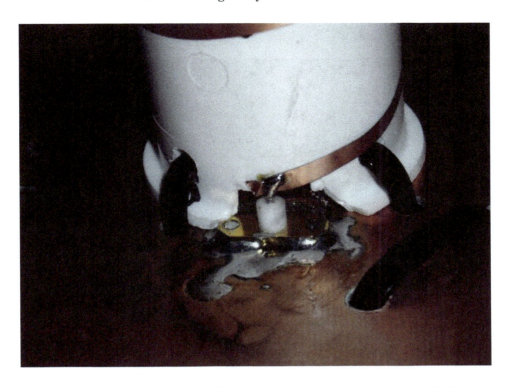

The feedpoint connection: solder the center conductor to copper foil tape.

2. Attach the angle bracket and wifi adapter, making sure all parts are secure and ready for service, as seen in the images below.

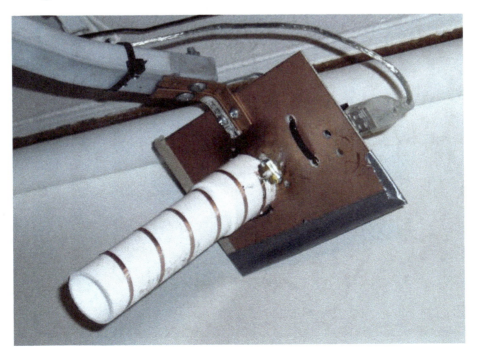

Short wifi helix feeding a long range parabolic wifi antenna.

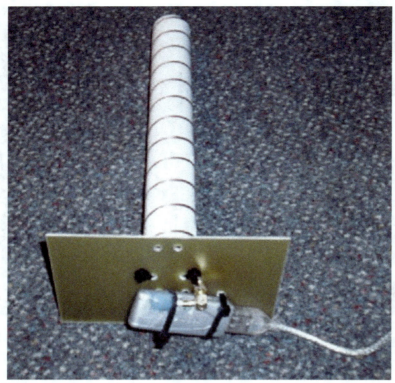

Cable losses are avoided by mounting wifi adapter at base of antenna.

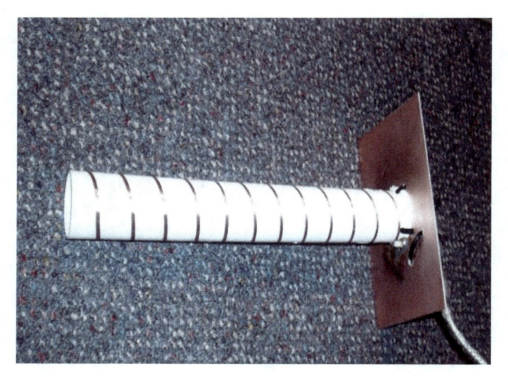

The bigger 10 turn helical wifi antenna.

With the helix built and parts installed, the antenna is ready for a smoke test. If you can apply some wifi to it, and the smoke stays inside your wifi dongle, all is good. If the smoke escapes and you see or smell it, something is wrong...

First, plug in the cables and look for some signals! Theoretical gain of the prototype helical was about 18 dB over an isotropic radiator; it beat my biquad by about 7 to 13 RSSI units, and indeed seemed less sensitive to polarization and rainfall. Signals still seem to fluctuate much from second to second. If your antenna is functioning satisfactorily at this point, I suggest spray painting three layers of clearcoat onto the windings and groundplane for stability and corrosion prevention.

Notes: _____

_____

_____

_____

_____

# Long and Longer Yagi Antennas

Constructing a wifi yagi antenna is a great way to get some gain on your classic signals quickly and you do not need a lot of tools, dishes, or to work with sheet metal. It will greatly extend your ability to reach 802.11abgn access points. A well built yagi handily beats the single dipoles or collinear antennas boxed with a lot of wifi dongles.

I don't suggest the yagi if you are using wifi6 or wifi7. Newer wifi types as these operate on multiple bands, with internal antennas designed for them. Also, the signal modes are superior – much more robust and noise resistant. For long haul wifi6 or wifi7, set up a parabolic dish, dongle, and Single Board Computer to pump a flood of zeros and ones down some ethernet cable. Build a yagi for wifi if you are on a classic device or simply want to experiment and poke about your local 2.4 GHz band.

When connected to a typical USB wireless adapter as a replacement for the stock antenna, the performance is excellent. When connected to a high powered wifi adapter, the yagi enables connectivity throughout an urban neighborhood or kilometers up and down the rural roads. Do not waste time building wifi cantennas - they don't perform anywhere close to the yagi antennas depicted here.

## That familiar reminder about using suitable wifi hardware...

Note that if your goal is to get wireless internet from another location and use it indoors, you should instead consider using a wireless bridge. If you want to provide strong wireless internet coverage to an outdoor area, but cannot provide a fiber optic or ethernet cable to your wireless router, again consider using a wireless bridge to substitute for the unavailable cable, and connect the bridge to the router. This is a better solution for situations such as these:

- Providing internet connectivity from one building to users in a remote house or office.

- Providing internet connectivity from one highrise building to another across town.

- Providing internet connectivity from an onshore location to users on an island.

- Sharing connectivity between two locations which can't be linked by cable.

 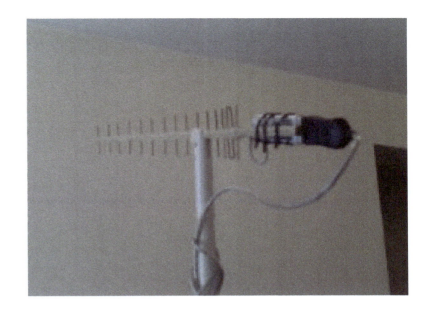

Reach hotspots via window mounting. Connect through concrete walls.

Let's start with a look at the software I started this adventure with: the W9CF yagi antenna modeler, written in Java. It is quite a fine bit of software, which is not only fast, but considers metal element diameter conductivity, element spacing and tapering techniques. It Draws a diagram of the antenna pattern, physical set-up, and creates a table of element spacings and lengths.

Notes: _____

_____

_____

_____

_____

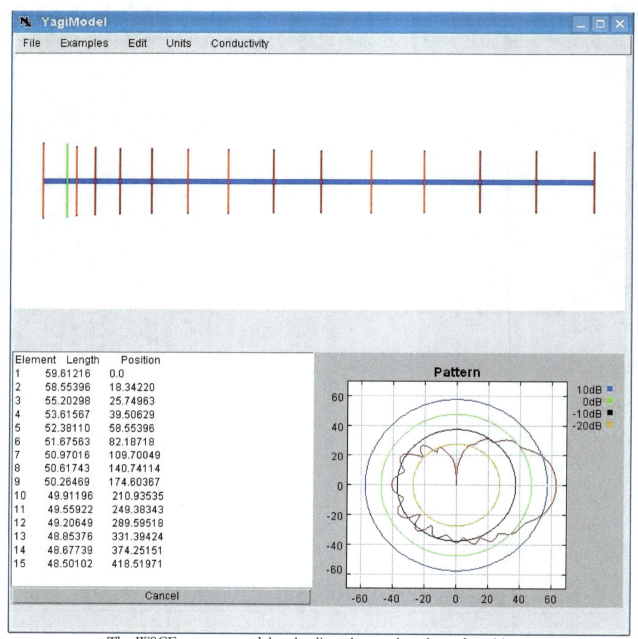

The W9CF antenna modeler also lists element lengths and positions.

The yagi wifi antenna design depicted here can be built in just an hour or two, and it works great! It is made of wood and wire and provides high gain and directivity. It is directional - favoring wi-fi signals in one direction and rejecting interference from the sides or behind the antenna. The 15 element wi-fi antenna provides over 15 dB of gain (multiplying your effective radiated power by 31), while the larger 20 element wifi antenna provides over 17 dB of gain (multiplying your effective radiated power power by 51). Front to back ratio for both antennas is about 22 dB.

Yagi wifi antennas are not very forgiving of inaccurate design and construction, but this one works fine if you measure and cut precisely. Use calipers and a magnifier if you must, but keep the errors under a millimeter. When cutting wire, cut a millimeter long and file down the ends to make sure that the lengths are correct.

The W9CF antenna modeler initially starts with several examples tailored for operation in the amateur radio bands. One of the best designs is the classic K1FO yagi. By following a few steps, the antenna can be scaled for the 2.4 Ghz wifi 802.11 b/g/n frequencies:

1.  Start with the 15 or 20 element K1FO 70cm example.

2.  In the "units" menu, select "Radians."

3.  In the "conductivity" menu, select "Copper"

4.  In the "frequency" field, enter 2450 (MHz) for the center of the wifi networking band.

5.  For "Element Diameter", enter 0.08729 (radians).

6.  Click the "calculate" button.

7.  In the "units" menu, select "millimeters."

8.  Note that the element diameter perfectly matches 14 gauge wire!

9.  In the file menu, select "list elements."

The elements list will show each antenna element, from the reflector (element 1, position zero mm), to the last director. Do not use a different metal or a different diameter of metal for the elements, or performance will suffer. **That's 14 awg copper wire, no paperclips!** Changes in element diameter, metal type, or design frequency will need recalculation and the generation of a new elements list. Use the dimensions in the table below.

Note: As of this writing, in April 2022, the original antenna modeler seems to no longer be available for download. There is another very good calculator running on a web page, producing a design based on the DL6WU yagi. See Appendix 2 for an example calculated for the 2.4 GHz wifi band.

# Element data for the 15 Element Yagi Wifi Antenna:

| Element | Length (mm) | Position (mm) |
|---|---|---|
| 1 (Reflector) | 59.61 | 0.00 |
| 2 (Driven Element) | 58.55 | 18.34 |
| 3 (Director) | 55.20 | 25.75 |
| 4 (Director) | 53.62 | 39.51 |
| 5 (Director) | 52.38 | 58.55 |
| 6 (Director) | 51.68 | 82.19 |
| 7 (Director) | 50.97 | 109.70 |
| 8 (Director) | 50.62 | 140.74 |
| 9 (Director) | 50.26 | 174.60 |
| 10 (Director) | 49.91 | 210.94 |
| 11 (Director) | 49.56 | 249.38 |
| 12 (Director) | 49.21 | 289.60 |
| 13 (Director) | 48.85 | 331.39 |
| 14 (Director) | 48.68 | 374.25 |
| 15 (Director) | 48.50 | 418.52 |

Plan views of the yagis are included below, meticulously adapted by the author from the modeling software, showing element lengths and positions along the boom, measured from the reflector. The reference datum is the reflector element, designated as location 00 millimeters.

Note that the driven element is depicted in green. It is actually a folded dipole. Why a folded dipole? It provides a good impedance match to coaxial cable when used as the yagi wifi antenna's driven element. In free space, a folded dipole has a 300 ohm impedance at resonance, but the impedance drops drastically when placed in a yagi, due to the increased current caused by the resonant reflector and director elements.

There are better ways to match the antenna impedance to the transmission line from the wifi dongle. They would, however, make the antenna more complex to build and create more opportunities for for performance problems if the matching is not perfect.

Notes: _____

_____

_____

_____

_____

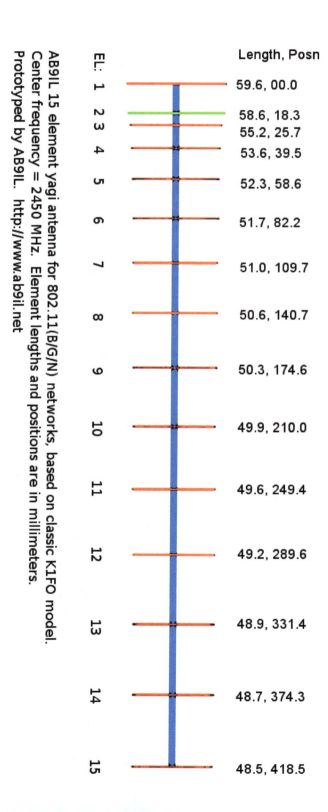

Length, Posn

| EL: | Length, Posn |
|-----|--------------|
| 1 | 59.6, 00.0 |
| 2 | 58.6, 18.3 |
| 3 | 55.2, 25.7 |
| 4 | 53.6, 39.5 |
| 5 | 52.3, 58.6 |
| 6 | 51.7, 82.2 |
| 7 | 51.0, 109.7 |
| 8 | 50.6, 140.7 |
| 9 | 50.3, 174.6 |
| 10 | 49.9, 210.0 |
| 11 | 49.6, 249.4 |
| 12 | 49.2, 289.6 |
| 13 | 48.9, 331.4 |
| 14 | 48.7, 374.3 |
| 15 | 48.5, 418.5 |

AB9IL 15 element yagi antenna for 802.11(B/G/N) networks, based on classic K1FO model.
Center frequency = 2450 MHz.  Element lengths and positions are in millimeters.
Prototyped by AB9IL.  http://www.ab9il.net

# Element data for the 20 Element Yagi Wifi Antenna:

| Element | Length (mm) | Position (mm) |
|---|---|---|
| 1 (Reflector) | 59.96 | 0.00 |
| 2 (Driven Element) | 58.91 | 18.34 |
| 3 (Director) | 55.56 | 25.75 |
| 4 (Director) | 53.97 | 39.51 |
| 5 (Director) | 52.73 | 58.55 |
| 6 (Director) | 52.03 | 82.19 |
| 7 (Director) | 51.32 | 109.70 |
| 8 (Director) | 50.97 | 140.74 |
| 9 (Director) | 50.61 | 174.60 |
| 10 (Director) | 50.26 | 210.94 |
| 11 (Director) | 49.91 | 249.38 |
| 12 (Director) | 49.56 | 289.60 |
| 13 (Director) | 49.21 | 331.39 |
| 14 (Director) | 49.03 | 374.25 |
| 15 (Director) | 48.85 | 418.52 |
| 16 (Director) | 48.68 | 463.67 |
| 17 (Director) | 48.50 | 509.70 |
| 18 (Director) | 48.32 | 556.26 |
| 19 (Director) | 48.15 | 603.53 |

20 (Director)                  47.97                      651.32

Notes: _____

_____

_____

_____

_____

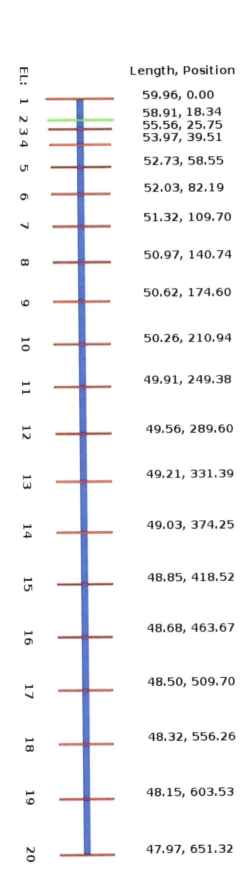

El: 1 2 3 4 5 6 7 8 9 10 11 12 13 14 15 16 17 18 19 20

Length, Position

59.96, 0.00
58.91, 18.34
55.56, 25.75
53.97, 39.51
52.73, 58.55
52.03, 82.19
51.32, 109.70
50.97, 140.74
50.62, 174.60
50.26, 210.94
49.91, 249.38
49.56, 289.60
49.21, 331.39
49.03, 374.25
48.85, 418.52
48.68, 463.67
48.50, 509.70
48.32, 556.26
48.15, 603.53
47.97, 651.32

A 20 element yagi antenna for 802.11(B/G/N) networks, based on classic K1FO model. Center frequency = 2450 MHz. Element lengths and positions are in millimeters. Prototyped by AB9IL. http://www.ab9il.net

Construction of this requires some measuring, cutting, bending, and bolting of metal. Use caution around the sharp edges. When finished, put it up and enjoy a very durable antenna that provides outstanding wifi performance.

## Yagi wifi antenna parts list:

1. A 1.2 meter length of 14 AWG bare, solid copper wire.

2. One wooden square, 1 cm per side, 50 cm long (70 cm for the 20 element antenna).

3. Wire cutters.

4. Metric ruler.

5. Drill, with 1.6 mm (1/16") bit.

6. Printed or written template with antenna dimensions.

7. Ball point pen or fine felt tipped marker.

## Yagi wifi antenna construction:

Assemble the yagi wifi antenna following the steps below, starting with preparation of the boom, followed by mounting the elements. After the elements are mounted, a suitable connector is added, and the antenna is tested over-the-air. Keep in mind that it can be connected to most usb wireless adapters by cutting the circuit board antenna trace and patching in a pigtail feeding the antenna.

1. Draw a line as accurately as possible down the center of one side of the wooden boom.

2. Mark the boom centerline 5 cm from one end. This is the "zero location," where the director element will be mounted.

3. Continue down the boom, carefully marking the locations of each element on the centerline.

4. Carefully drill through the boom at each element's location. Make sure to drill straight through the boom, emerging on the other side still centered and perpendicular.

5. For a no-drill alternative, carefully cut a perpendicular groove across the boom, to a depth of 2 mm.

6. Cut one element at a time, carefully measuring each element before and after cutting, trimming as necessary for proper length. File the wire ends

and make sure the lengths are as accurate as possible!

7.  Press elements through the boom, centering each before moving to the next element.

8.  If you cut grooves for the elements instead of drilling holes, press the elements down into the grooves, and make sure each is straight and centered. Affix them permanently with epoxy.

Element positions marked on the yagi wifi antenna boom.

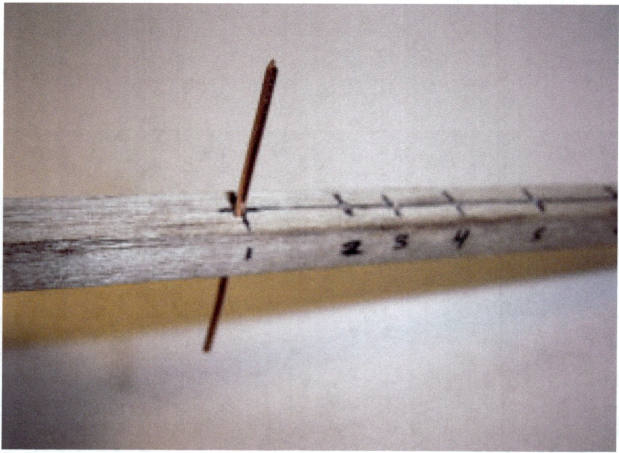

The
reflector element after mounting.

9.  For the driven element, cut a 130 mm length of wire, and make a 180 degree bend 30 mm from one end. Mount in boom, then make a bend 30 mm from other end. Adjust as necessary to create a folded dipole just under 59 mm in length with 5 mm spacing.

10. Double check all elements, making sure all are centered and parallel.

11. Attach a pigtail (or connector) to open ends of folded dipole.

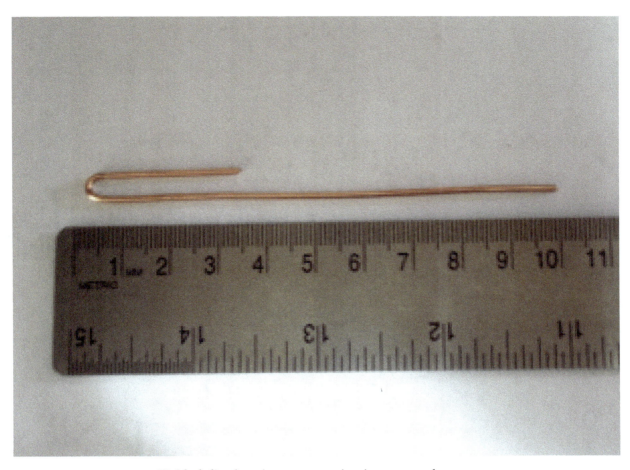

Folded dipole prior to mounting in antenna boom.

<grin>That's 14 awg solid copper wire, not a paperclip.

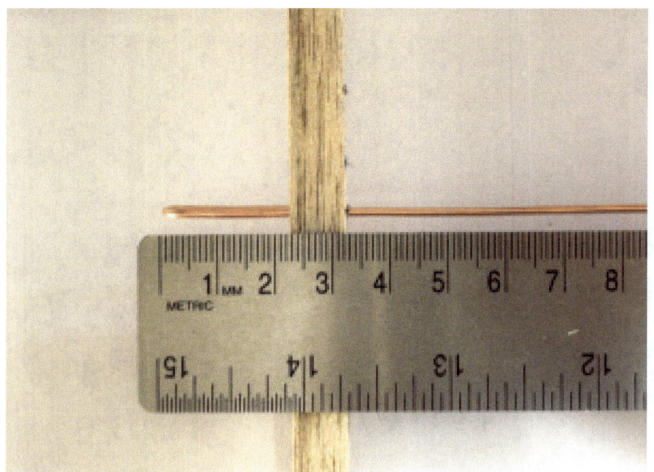

The driven element before the last bend.

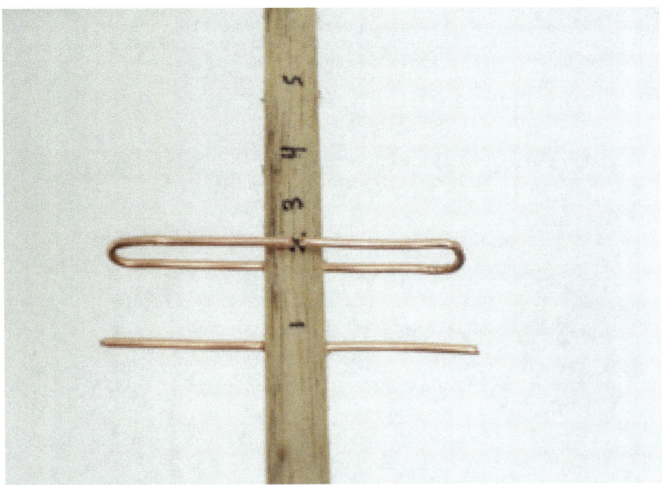

Two yagi wifi antenna elements mounted in boom.

After all of the elements are measured, cut, and mounted, the antenna should resemble the finished yagi pictured below. Connect the pigtail or connector to the driven element. Then connect the wifi adapter or wireless router to the antenna and start checking over-the-air signal strengths. Note that the antenna may be sensitive to polarization: when the antenna seems to bring in the best signal, rotate it to find the best polarization. Mounting the antenna is possible using commonly available hardware, such as 90 degree angle brackets, U bolts, or even velcro.

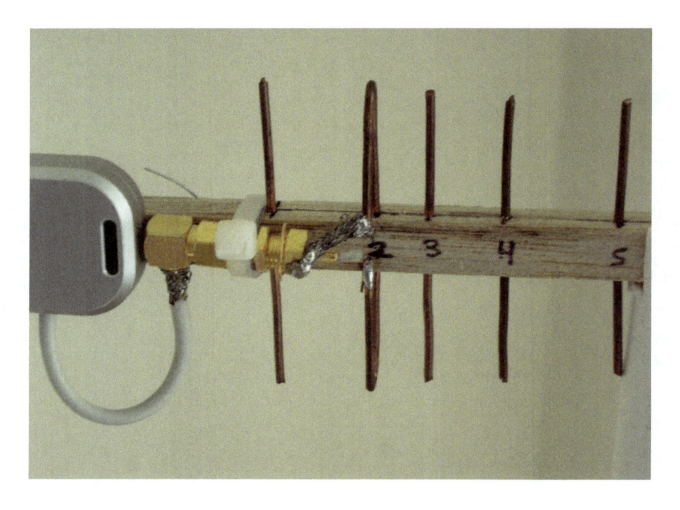

Closeup of the wifi yagi feedpoint. Keep the leads short!

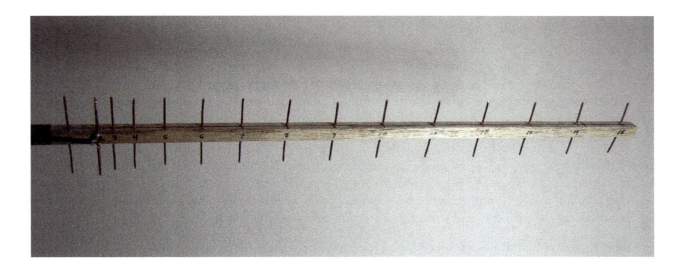

The completed wifi yagi antenna.

## Yagi wifi antenna testing:

For the most practical method of signal checking, consider using a wifi auditing utility such as Kismet or Aircrack-ng. Either of these will produce a rapidly updated received signal strength indication that is useful for comparing or aiming wifi directional antennas. Make a set of measurements for any desired wi fi access points on the original antenna, then make a new set for the yagi antenna. I have built several of these over the years, and they sure work nicely.

Notes: _____

_____

_____

_____

# Yagis for Extended Access Point Range

Many techniques of wireless network range enhancement focus on the use of high gain antennas at client end of the link. For example, the wifi yagi seen on this page has been used for years on a USB wireless adapter. It allowed me to move about a nearby park and coffee shop and still connect to my home network. Others have used the wifi yagi at distances of kilometers over open space. Generally, the access points were using wireless routers equipped with simple dipole antennas, and the yagi was quite necessary for full bandwidth connections beyond about 70 meters (and less indoors or in an interference filled environment).

Be aware that if your goal is to get wireless internet from another location and use it indoors, you should instead consider using a wireless bridge. If you want to provide strong wireless internet coverage to an area, but cannot provide a fiber optic or ethernet cable to your wireless router, again consider using a wireless bridge to substitute for the unavailable cable, and connect the bridge to the router.

In the long distance wifi router project shown here, a high gain wifi yagi antenna was used for greatly increasing the range and effectiveness of an access point. The author was able to connect, through interference, and enjoy broadband internet connections at a distance of 300 meters. A laptop was used as the client, without any other special antennas. In another test, wifi yagis with about 15 dB gain were used at both ends, and connections were possible at a distance of 1.5 km. In a more open, noise free environment, the yagi to yagi wi-fi link should be usable over several km. Connections are especially stable and fast if a high power wifi router is used at the access point.

A yagi on a router provides strong signals and long distance coverage.

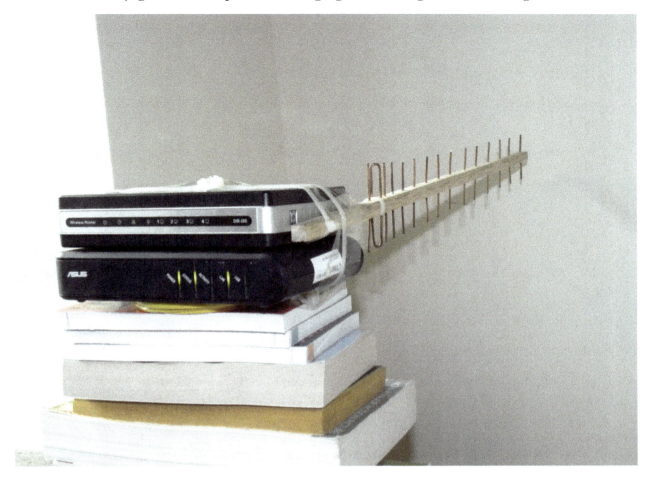

Penetrate concrete walls by using a wireless router - yagi combination.

Avoid aiming through walls to access outdoor users; walls greatly weaken wifi signals. As much as 30dB is lost per wall!! Find a window or mount the equipment outdoors in a weatherproof container.

## Build the wifi yagi and connect it to a wireless router.

This project is a relatively simple matter of replacing the router's mediocre dipole antenna with the yagi. You need the following supplies:

1. One wireless router, with an external antenna connector.

2. One coaxial pigtail, compatible with the router. Note that the cable is deliberately short to minimize signal losses.

3. A wifi yagi antenna. Build or buy one. You do need a high gain antenna on your router!

4. Duct tape or cable ties (they're non-metallic) for securing the pigtail and antenna.

To assemble the high gain antenna and router combination, accomplish the following steps:

1. Solder the pigtail to the antenna driven element. Center conductor to one side and shield to the other

2. Secure the pigtail with one or two cable ties, preventing movement and breakage

3. Replace the wireless router's dipole with the wifi yagi antenna.

4. Use tape and / or cable ties to secure the antenna to the router and prevent movement and breakage.

## Carefully mount and aim the wifi antenna / router combination.

The wireless router / high gain antenna assembly should be directed toward the area to be used by intended clients. It can be aimed through walls for enhanced indoor coverage or placed by a window and aimed towards distant users outdoors. There is also a usable signal outside of the beam for distances within about 10 meters.

Another mounting option, if very high quality / low loss coaxial cable is available, is to mount the antenna on a wall or other fixed structure, and run a length of coaxial cable to the router, affixed securely nearby. Run no more than one meter of cable! The shorter the better.

Most classic wifi routers are equipped with mediocre dipole antennas. Replace them with high gain units for longer access point range.

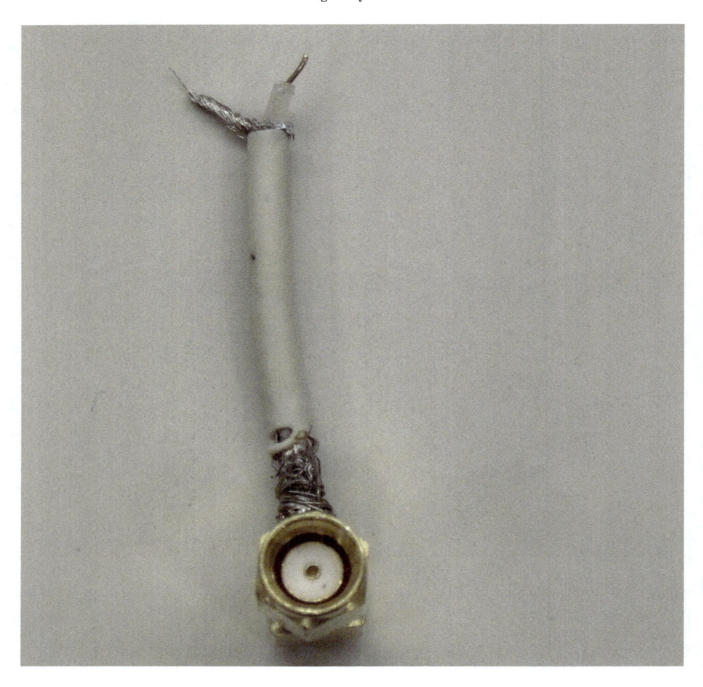

The coaxial pigtail has a compatible connector and is as short as possible, to reduce losses.

The Ultimate Big Crazy Wifi Antenna Guide

This high gain wireless router antenna is affixed to the router with cable ties and tape. Okay for indoor use.

# Aspects of High Power / High Gain Wifi

The combination of moderate to high power wireless routers and high gain antennas make possible the coverage of large areas with broadband wireless networks. The improved radiated power and increased sensitivity add up to a number of extra decibels of strength above the minimum needed, as measured in the area served. That is "link budget" in a nutshell, and the important thing about the router fattening the link budget, is that weaker devices – smart phones, tablets, and laptop computers, will connect better than they otherwise would.

Over longer distances, more decibels are lost, and the hardware must be more performant to meet the minimum link budget necessary to make a connection. Wireless connectivity is possible over extreme distances when high gain antennas and higher power are used on both ends of the link.

When considering using high power wifi devices to cover large areas, some thought should be given to determining the actual needs for the link in question. How much power is required for a good connection? Can transmitter power alone do the job, or must a directional antenna also be used? Is the area wide open, or will the wireless signals have to go through walls, floors, or shrubs? Are there other strong wifi signals or noise sources which must be overcome?

## The Long Tail of Signal Strength

Consider a scenario of a person intending to connect to their wireless network over a large area - a farm, marina, or warehouse - with walls and floors between the user and wireless router. Perhaps the wireless access point currently peaks at 6 Mbps speed and the question is how to increase throughput. Faster wireless requires stronger signals, but how much stronger? The answer comes through figuring a "link budget."

Think of your typical wireless adapter, and how it's maximum connection speed increases with signal strength. Using the Alfa AWUS036H wireless adapter as an example of a sensitive device, a -85 dBm signal is needed for 9 Mbps and -71 dBm for a full 54 Mbps. See the table below:

# ALFA AWUS036H Data Rate Vs Signal Strength

| Signal Strength | Data Rate | Modulation Mode |
| --- | --- | --- |
| -71dBm | 54Mpbs | 64QAM |
| -76dBm | 48 Mbps | 64QAM |
| -78dBm | 36Mpbs | 16QAM |
| -80dBm | 24 Mbps | 16QAM |
| -81dBm | 18 Mbps | QPSK |
| -82dBm | 12Mpbs | QPSK |
| -85dBm | 9 Mbps | BPSK |
| -91dBm | 6 Mbps | BPSK |

At the other end of the link the access point may be running a typical 100mw, which translates to +20dBm. Assume both wifi radios are initially using those mediocre little dipoles included with the devices when purchased, and the Alfa is receiving the distant AP at a signal strength of -91dBm. Expect a slow 6 Mbps connection. Okay for email, but not YouTube!! The cumulative losses of antenna cables, terrain, distance, and other factors have reduced the signal by 111 dB between the circuit board in the wireless access point to the receiver board in the Alfa AWUS036H. The Alfa, on the other hand, has a transmit power up to 27dBm, and would put about -84 dBm into the wireless access point. The AWUS036H can probably transmit beyond its receive range, considering the power of typical APs.

If a faster connection is desired, more signal will have to be focused on the path with a high gain wifi antenna. A yagi or parabolic on one end of the link could provide a gain of 15 dB, making 36 Mbps to 48 Mbps connections possible. High gain antennas at both ends of the link would easily add 25dB to 30dB to the link, and make full speed 54 Mbps connectivity a reality. That is much better than a paltry 6 Mbps connection under the original conditions.

Will higher power make more wireless access points available? Yes. Look at the signal survey below. It represents a typical population of wireless access points in an urban location, receiving from a 2nd floor window:

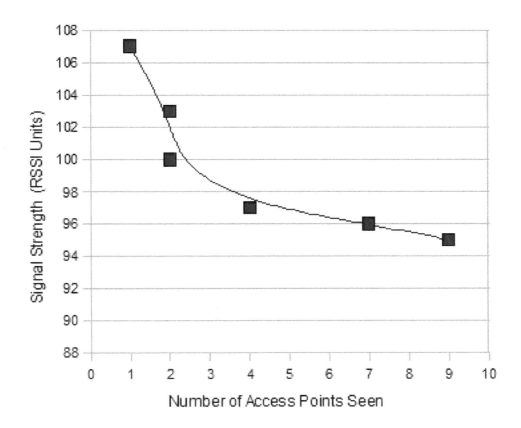

There were only 3 very strong APs (above 102 RSSI units) in view. However, the "long tail" contained another 22 weaker access points! Some of those weak ones could be reachable with high gain wifi antennas and high power wifi interfaces. Not only would the population shown in the chart be reachable "short tail" statistics; a whole new population of "long tail" signals would appear. When using high power wifi interfaces, directional antennas would actually be necessary to limit interference from nearby unwanted sources.

## Finding High Power Wifi Hardware

If possible, use a high power wireless router to provide internet access in an office, home, or open space. Also consider using a suitable antenna for the area to be covered. Omnidirectional antennas may be best for large areas surrounding the access point; a dish or yagi antenna may be more suitable if the access point serves users in one general direction. When the access point is putting out the strongest possible signal, the next level of refinement is up to power and antennas on the client end of the link.

The well known and well engineered Alfa AWUS036H has been mentioned already as a high power wireless adapter, running up to 27dBm / 500mw. It isn't the only device available, however, and the competition is heating up. The EnGenius EUB9603h is a high power, 600mW, 802.11bgn USB wireless adapter that also accepts an external antenna. Imagine the range available if that device is connected to a high gain wifi dish or high gain wifi yagi antenna!

A Google search for high power wireless reveals plenty of excellent interfaces. Ubiquiti and Data-Alliance are notables offering high power wifi adapters in the form of PCI and Mini-PCI cards, though they may not be be best for all computers, as some laptops lack ability to fully power these devices. When in doubt, use USB wireless adapters; power is then not an issue.

At the time of this writing, I notice that several USB wifi adapters are listed on web retailers Newegg and Amazon, with still more available through Aliexpress. There seems to be less emphasis on high transmit power, due to the superior modulation methods of 802.11ax and low interference levels on the new 5 and 6 GHz bands. Mist have internal, self contained antennas. A few have antennas which may be unfolded for use.

Here are some suggestions for getting the most out of wifi 5, wifi 6, and wifi 7:

- Broadband wifi needs to be fed broadband ethernet. Subscribe, if you can, to "gigabit service" from your ISP and use fiber or Cat 6 ethernet to distribute internet within your home or office.

- Mount your access points where you would mount lights: high on walls, centered on ceilings, etc.

- Avoid situations where you would try to get wifi through walls. Instead, go through the trouble to run ethernet to the enclosed location.

- Use wifi mesh networking to cover large areas, and consider adding one or two extra nodes to cover and fill in your busy areas.

# Wireless Network Security Issues

Wireless networking is convenient, fast, and provides a lot of computing mobility. Wifi does, however, require extra measures if it is to be as secure as hard-wired networks. Avoid operating in the clear or using basic WPA. WPA2 is the standard to use at this time (2022).

Encryption not only protects your data, it prevents trouble makers from getting onto your network and using it to launch or manage evil acts across the internet. Make your password long and unique, as even WPA2 will fail to protect against weak passwords.

Surveillance of Wireless Networks

Consider for a moment the number of wireless networks visible to a laptop in a good wifi location. There is probably a small number of strong signals, and a larger number of fair signals, and a large number of weak (but readable)signals. Anyone with software and hardware capable of monitoring the airwaves can capture wireless data and subject it to analysis. In some ways, WiFi is similar to the telephone party lines of long ago, when it was possible to simply listen and gather information on the other people with access to the line. Woe unto the person giving up sensitive data over such a channel. It really is an important matter considering the "long tail" population of fair to weak networks that are perhaps too weak for connections, but still strong enough to tap from far away! Plenty of weak 802.11 signals are yet strong enough for surveillance!

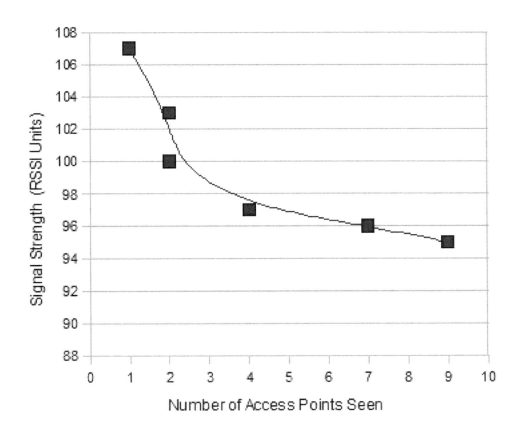

For a long time, up to the early 2000s, the popular solution to keeping wireless network data safe from prying eyes was Wired Equivalent Privacy (WEP). It provided a means of securing communications in the age of Intel 486 processors. Smarter attack methods and more powerful PCs rendered it ineffective. If your network is still using WEP, you are as vulnerable to surveillance as if you used no encryption. Stop using WEP and switch to WPA2, with a long and random password.

WEP's weakness is in its tendency to leak data about the encryption key, which can be used to break the key in a matter of minutes. In essence, the attacker captures all traffic on the network, then applies a statistical algorithm to determine the key. When the key is broken, the attacker may use the network infrastructure and has access to its data. One can then monitor all users' surfing habits, collect passwords, and carry out other malicious activities.

The safer encryption protocol is WiFi Protected Access v2 (WPA2). It uses a more secure scheme for managing keys, and is orders of magnitude more resistant to cryptanalysis. One essential requirement with WPA2 is to select a password that is NOT composed of known words that can be found in a dictionary, as there have been demonstrations of WPA1 keys being "reverse engineered" to poor key selection by end users. It is that password which, along with the network SSID, used as seed to produce one very long and tough to crack hash as the wireless crypto key. Attackers essentially precompute keys (once) using common SSIDs and dictionary words, and build "rainbow tables" to simply look up the keys (any number of times).

With fast solid state drives, dozens of gigabytes of memory, and powerful CPU / GPU combinations, weak keys or passwords fail quickly. Quick enough that you should take this seriously.

## Countermeasures Against Wifi Network Surveillance

No cryptosystem is totally secure; the best simply take more time and resources to break than the attackers are willing to sacrifice. The smartest policy is to keep sensitive data off the network, and use WPA2 if the network must be used for semi-sensitive data. For more reading on the recent advances in cryptanalysis of WPA, see Practical attacks against WEP and WPA2 by Beck and Tews.

Sometimes there simply isn't a secure wireless network available. In addition, very sensitive data should always be hidden from wireless hackers, dictatorial authorities, and institutions disrespecting individual privacy. Excellent data security is available in the form of Virtual Private Networking (VPN). A VPN is a service which protects data by creating an encrypted channel between the user's computer and a trusted server in a different location. The VPN server is the user's connection point to the internet, and the user's IP address reflects that trusted server's location. Passing network traffic through a VPN makes it impossible for an institution or government to restrict a user's internet access, sniff sensitive data, or track a user's browsing. VPN can also provide anonymity superior to that offered by popular web based proxy services. It is important to realize that a VPN acts as a "secure network interface" and protects the flow of all data in and out of the computer - not merely web browser activity. FTP, VOIP, and other non-browser data are protected.

In addition to VPNs, users should use more secure web browser settings:

- Set the browser to favor https over plain http, and allow the browser to show an annoying alert whenever there is an attempt to load a page using plain http.

- Use DNS over https or DNS over TLS. This prevents monitoring or tampering with the nameserver lookup process.

- Use Encrypted Server Name Indication (SNI), which prevents an attacker from reading your browser history.

- When available, use end to end encryption for messaging and cloud services.

Whether you are a telecommuter working from home, a journalist writing an expose on your government's misuse of power, or simply a person doing online banking, consider protecting yourself and your work by using WPA2 for wireless and VPN for all networking. On top of that, use hardened web browser settings.

## WiFi Man In The Middle Attacks

We would all like to think that the wifi networks we use are secure and that the promise of secure mobile connectivity is fully realized. The truth is that mobility, security, and convenience are all in measures, and that some measures are greater than others. And some measures are nil. For secure computing in a mobile or portable environment it is essential to observe certain effective precautions, because there are entities seeking to capture and use your sensitive data.

## Defining the "Man in the Middle" Scenario

A Man In The Middle attack, often abbreviated as MITM, is accomplished by inserting a third party into a two party communication and hiding that fact from the original two participants. The man in the middle then gets access to the data and can secretly alter it for his own purposes.

Imagine Alice and Bob, a century ago, communicating via paper notes. The evil character Madison is a master of counterfeit with access to their letters while enroute. Madison reads their letters and passes them on unaltered. Then one day Bob offers to buy Alice's valuable collection of antique office furniture. Alice agrees, and requests payment info with a delivery address. Bob sends his banking and delivery information, but Madison alters it all. Madison gives Alice the address of his stolen goods dealer, and he transfers all of Bob's money into an offshore account. Madison sends Bob an authentic looking note from Alice indicating that all is well and to expect delivery in four more days. Not to happen! Alice and Bob have been duped by an impostor middleman who will have vanished before any suspicion arises.

Or, imagine a secret business transaction between A and B, carried out via a courier trusted by both sides who actually is an agent for a third company, C. The transaction stalls because the courier alters the terms seen by A or B, and makes them unreasonable. The company C comes along and clinches the deal thanks to middleman sabotage. A and B have no idea that their offers were rewritten enroute.

Note: There are non-free countries where internet users are required to have their web browsers set up to use state controlled security certificates for browsing SSL encrypted pages! If you are in such a place, the authorities can decrypt your web traffic. Beware, that it does not matter if you have nothing to hide: It is not your responsibility to give up information that is no one else's business. The power of search and seizure must always be used for just cause and never arbitrarily.

## "Man in the Middle" Wifi Version

In wireless networking, the MITM scheme is implemented in a number of ways. One is to operate a rogue access point resembling a legitimate wireless hotspot. Often the real access point is jammed or blocked while the rogue, with the same SSID, is in the clear with a strong signal. Another method is to break a client's connection and lure the client's hardware into reconnecting to the middleman. In this case the middleman has faked the access point MAC address.

Be aware that these attacks are not limited to wireless networks; there have been cases of proxy servers (and even the TOR network) faking security for SSL / HTTPS communications. It means that banking, secure email, and other sensitive connections have been compromised by man in the middle schemes. The intent again is to access and use or alter confidential data passed on a network.

## Countermeasures Against "Man in the Middle" Attacks

What protections are there against man in the middle attacks on your network? Consider these steps:

1. Survey the APs operating with your unique SSID. Take down any that are not authorized to be on the air.

2. Use strong encryption on your network. WPA2 is much better than WEP

3. Use SSL. It will make man in the middle attacks more difficult, and will prevent most attacks.

4. Double check SSL certificates before using https pages. IE and Firefox can do this for you.

5. Encrypt any documents you don't want to be intercepted or altered.

6. Using a VPN service is quite effective against man in the middle attacks

7. Forget about WEP and original WPA. They are easy to break. Use WPA2 encryption

In conclusion remember that no communications security system is 100.000% secure. Successful ones require so much effort to break that the information is worthless by the time it is extracted and used. Your best policy is to limit the flow of sensitive information, off the network, and use the strongest possible protection. For more reading about rogue access points and man in the middle attacks, see Rogue Access Points and the University of British Columbia Wifi Network.

The Ultimate Big Crazy Wifi Antenna Guide

# Belkin F5D7050 External Antenna

Many classic Wifi USB wireless adapters have very good electronics paired with rather poor antennas. While these devices are adequate for very local networking, they are capable of much better performance when connected to a high quality external antenna. The Belkin F5D7050 is a common device yet it can give uncommon range and speed performance with the modification described here.

Note: If you can't find this wifi device, there are newer high power wireless adapters and routers available. Get a new one, and connect!

Here is a project that can greatly increase wifi connection speed and range. It can be applied to just about any commonly available adapter; one simply cuts out the built in antenna and runs a feedline to a high gain replacement. I have seen throughput on a 30 meter path go from 5.5 MB/Sec to a solid 54 MB/Sec - with reduced interference and no need for amplification. Note that longer path lengths (more than 200 meters or through walls and vegetation) may require making this modification to a device higher powered than the F5D7050.

First, look at the circuit board. It boasts an efficient and clean layout. Data passes through the USB port on the left, and the antenna is etched on the right side. This modification is not difficult, but bright lighting and use of a magnifier is suggested due to the small surface mount parts and thin circuit traces on the adapter. It is a small work area, so use caution.

**Tools Needed:**

1. An X-Acto Knife or razor for cutting traces and trimming coaxial cable.

2. Soldering iron, with the tip sharpened, cleaned, and tinned.

3. One coaxial "pigtail" with connectors appropriate for antenna to be used.

4. Safety wire or epoxy for securing the pigtail to the PC board.

5.   Small drill if safety wiring will be used to secure the pigtail.

## F5D7050 Modification Procedure:

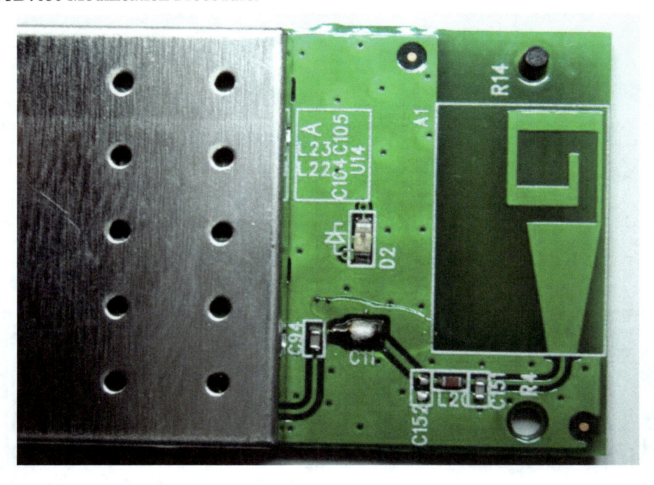

1.   Carefully pry open the adapter and remove it from its enclosure. Plan to work on the area to the right of the shielded circuitry.

2. Cut the printed circuit feedline between C11 and C152.

3. If wire will be used to hold down the pigtail, drill four small (1mm diam) holes in a square adjacent to the internal patch antenna.

4. Scrape away the coating over the ground plane in the area near C11 and D2.

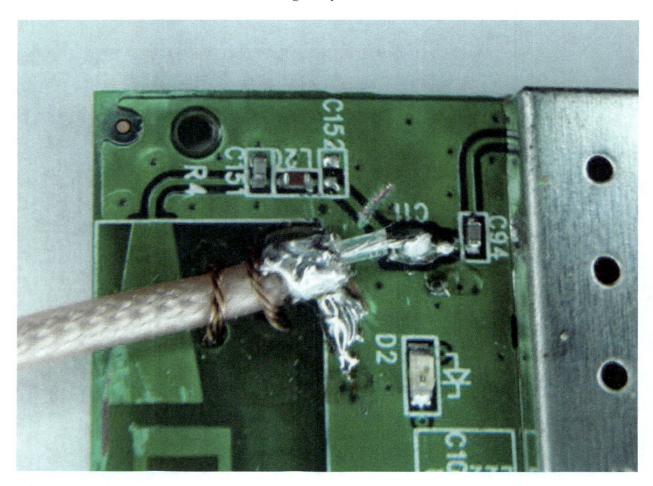

5.  Carefully prepare one end of the coaxial feedline for soldering to the board (keep it neat and avoid long leads).

6.  Connect the center conductor to C11; solder the shield to the ground plane.

7.  Wire or glue the pigtail to the circuit board. Make sure it will not flex or rip loose.

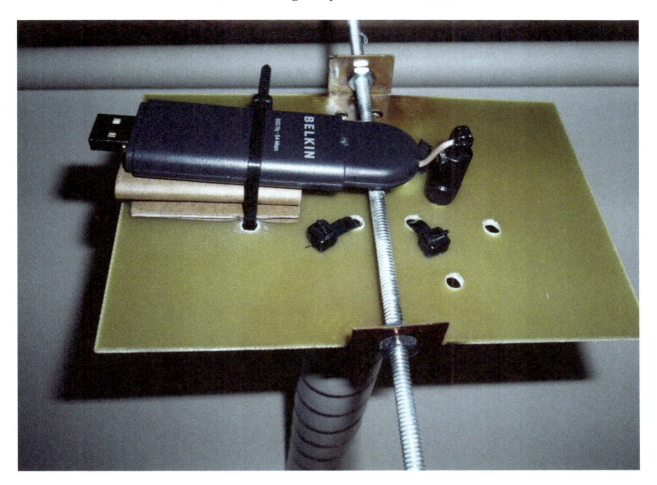

8. Carefully cut a gap into the enclosure to accommodate the pigtail, then re enclose the circuit.

9. Connect the adapter to the antenna; the modification is complete.

Notes: _____

_____

_____

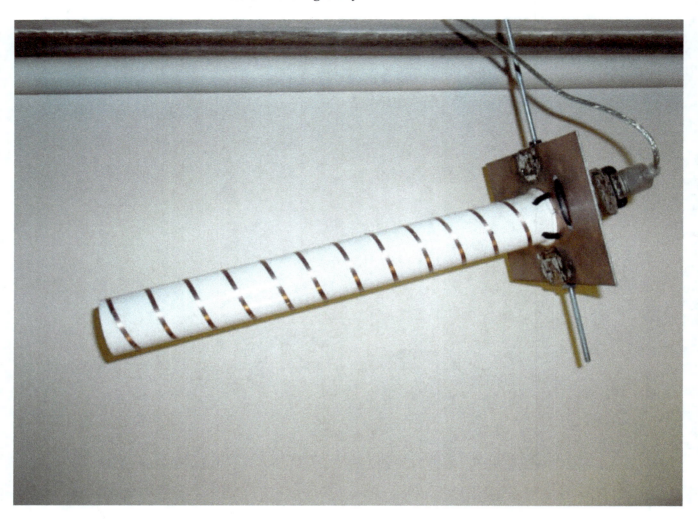

Above is an example of the modified F5D7050 and external antenna in operation. Some aiming will be necessary to peak the signal and maximize data rates. Performance of this USB wifi adapter went from good to outstanding with the added external antenna.

# Linksys WUSB54GC External Antenna

The Linksys WUSB54GC is a very good performer out of the box, thanks to a Ralink chipset and overall good design. It still has some limitations due to its internal antenna. With the addition of a good external antenna, it rises to excellence.

Note: If you can't find this wifi device, there are newer high power wireless adapters and routers available. Get a new one, and connect!

This project can greatly increase the throughput and range of the Linksys WUSB54GC. It can also be applied to just about any commonly available wifi adapter or router; one simply cuts out the built in antenna and runs coaxial cable to a high gain replacement. I have seen throughput on a 30 meter path go from 5.5 MB/Sec to a solid 54 MB/Sec - with reduced interference and no need for amplification. Note that longer path lengths (more than 200 meters or through walls and vegetation) may require making this modification to a device higher powered than the WUSB54GC.

First, look at the circuit board. It boasts an efficient and clean layout. Data passes through a USB port on the left, and the antenna is etched on the right side. This modification is not difficult, but bright lighting and use of a magnifier is suggested due to the small surface mount parts and thin circuit traces on the adapter. The WUSB54GC presents a small work area, so use caution.

The area for modification on the WUSB54GC

## Tools Needed:

1. An X-Acto Knife or razor for cutting traces and trimming coaxial cable.

2. Soldering iron, with the tip sharpened, cleaned, and tinned.

3. One coaxial "pigtail" with connectors appropriate for antenna to be used.

4. Safety wire or epoxy for securing the pigtail to the PC board.

5. Small drill if safety wiring will be used to secure the pigtail.

## Modification Procedure:

Pry open the adapter, remove it from its enclosure, work on the area to the right of the shielded circuitry. With the photos below as a guide, note the printed circuit stripline in the places marked in red.

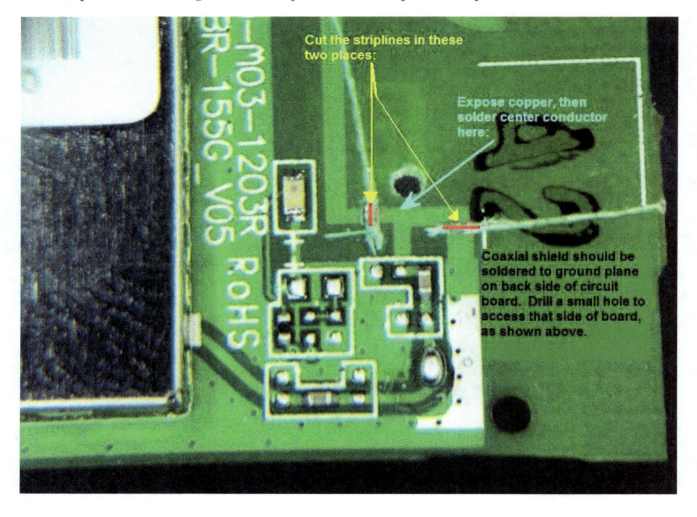

1. If wire will be used to hold down the pigtail, drill four small (1mm dia) holes in a square adjacent to the internal patch antenna.

2. Scrape away the coating over the ground plane in the area near the center conductor connection point.

3. Carefully prepare one end of the coaxial feedline for soldering to the board (keep it neat and avoid long leads).

4. Connect the center conductor to the "T" shaped tracing; solder the shield to the ground plane (consider drilling a hole to access the excellent groundplane on the back of the circuit board).

5. Wire or glue the pigtail to the circuit board. Make sure it will not flex or rip loose.

6. Carefully cut a gap into the enclosure to accommodate the pigtail, then re-enclose the circuit.

7. Connect the adapter to the antenna; the modification is complete.

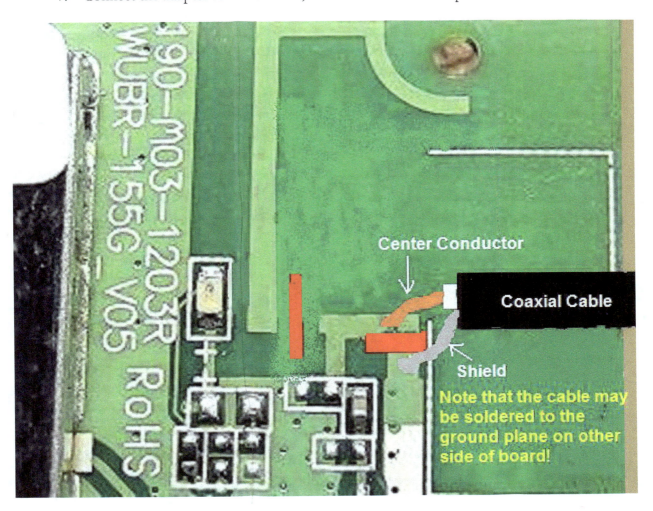

# Appendix I: Code Listings

Code listing for Python script "parabola.py"

Download at: https://gist.github.com/AB9IL/f0ff895f078f9fbd7c33f451208f4a02

```python
1  #!/usr/bin/python3
2
3  import matplotlib.pyplot as plt
4  import matplotlib.ticker as ticker
5  from math import sqrt, pow
6
7  # See see nicely written mathematical basis for
8  # defining the parabola and focus:
9  # http://physicsinsights.org/parabola_focus.html
10  # y is the axis of the parabola
11  # the directrix is below zero and parallels the x axis
12  # y = x**2  and also y = a * x***2 + b *x + c
13  # Keep it simple: make b and c equal to zero
14  # Work directly with the focus and compute the curve.
15
16  # parabola parameters
17  # the focus = f
18  f = 5
19  # set up some text
20  g = f + 2
21  text_1 = "  Focus: (0, " + str(f) + ")"
22  ##############################################################
23  # do not change these or you lose the parabolic curve
24  a = 1 / (4 * f)
```

```
25  b = 0

26  c = 0

27

28  # Descriptive text

29  i = f + 4

30  text_0 = "Parabola: " + str(a) + " * x^2 + " + str(b) + \

31      " * x " + "+ " + str(c)

32

33  # Defining the range of input values on the horizontal axis

34  x_values = [x for x in range(-12, 13)]

35

36  # Computing the values of the standard parabola

37  # for different values in x_values

38  y_values = [a * (pow(x, 2) + b * x + c) for x in x_values]

39

40  plt.style.use('seaborn-darkgrid')

41  fig, ax = plt.subplots()

42  ax.plot(x_values, y_values, linewidth=1)

43  ax.xaxis.set_major_locator(ticker.MultipleLocator(1))

44  ax.yaxis.set_major_locator(ticker.MultipleLocator(1))

45  plt.scatter(0, f)

46  plt.text(-8, i, text_0)

47  plt.text(-4, g, text_1)

48  plt.axis('square')

49                                          plt.show()
```

# Appendix II: An Alternate Yagi Calculator

Here is an alternate yagi calculator, available online, to replace the popular W9CF modeler. This one designs yagi antennas based on the DL6WU yagi, which has proven its value over decades in amateur and commercial radio service.

With thanks to Ajarn Changpuak, here is the calculator URL:

https://www.changpuak.ch/electronics/yagi_uda_antenna_DL6WU.php

Let us run the numbers for a long yagi:

      Frequency:    2450 MHz

      Elements:        20

      Element Diam:    2.5 mm      (3/32" brazing rod)

      Boom width:  7 mm      (insulated from elements)

If not using a wooden or fiberglass boom, the results are affected. Certainly, you may use aluminum or steel. Check "no" if parasitic elements are not insulated from the boom.

Results:

https://www.changpuak.ch/electronics/yagi_uda_antenna.php

Javascript Version 12.01.2014, based on Rothammel / DL6WU

---------------------------------------------------------------

| | |
|---|---|
| Frequency : | 2450 MHz |
| Wavelength : | 122 mm |
| Rod Diameter : | 2.5 mm |
| Boom Diameter : | 7 mm |
| Boom Length : | 744 mm |
| d/lambda : | 0.020 ( min.: 0.002 , max.: 0.01 ) |
| D/lambda : | 0.050 ( min.: 0.01 , max.: 0.05 ) |
| Elements : | 20 |

Gain        :          15.24 dBd (approx.)

------------------------------------------------------------

Reflector Length  :    59 mm

Reflector Position :    0 mm

------------------------------------------------------------

Dipole Position   :    29 mm

-----------------------------------------------------------

Director #1 Position :          39 mm , Length : 56 mm

Distance Dipole - Dir. #1 : 9 mm

-----------------------------------------------------------

Director #2 Position :          61 mm , Length : 55 mm

Distance Dir. #1 - Dir. #2 : 22 mm

-----------------------------------------------------------

Director #3 Position :          87 mm , Length : 55 mm

Distance Dir. #2 - Dir. #3 : 26 mm

-----------------------------------------------------------

Director #4 Position :          118 mm , Length : 54 mm

Distance Dir. #3 - Dir. #4 : 31 mm

-----------------------------------------------------------

Director #5 Position :          152 mm , Length : 54 mm

Distance Dir. #4 - Dir. #5 : 34 mm

-----------------------------------------------------------

Director #6 Position :          189 mm , Length : 53 mm

Distance Dir. #5 - Dir. #6 : 37 mm

-----------------------------------------------------------

Director #7 Position :          227 mm , Length : 53 mm

Distance Dir. #6 - Dir. #7 : 39 mm

-----------------------------------------------------------

Director #8 Position :          268 mm , Length : 53 mm

Distance Dir. #7 - Dir. #8 : 40 mm

-----------------------------------------------------------

Director #9 Position :          310 mm , Length : 52 mm

Distance Dir. #8 - Dir. #9 : 42 mm

-----------------------------------------------------------

Director #10 Position : 354 mm , Length : 52 mm

Distance Dir. #9 - Dir. #10 : 44 mm

-------------------------------------------------------------

Director #11 Position : 400 mm , Length : 52 mm

Distance Dir. #10 - Dir. #11 : 46 mm

-------------------------------------------------------------

Director #12 Position : 447 mm , Length : 52 mm

Distance Dir. #11 - Dir. #12 : 47 mm

-------------------------------------------------------------

Director #13 Position : 495 mm , Length : 52 mm

Distance Dir. #12 - Dir. #13 : 48 mm

------------------------------------------------------------

Director #14 Position : 543 mm , Length : 52 mm

Distance Dir. #13 - Dir. #14 : 48 mm

------------------------------------------------------------

Director #15 Position : 592 mm , Length : 51 mm

Distance Dir. #14 - Dir. #15 : 49 mm

------------------------------------------------------------

Director #16 Position : 641 mm , Length : 51 mm

Distance Dir. #15 - Dir. #16 : 49 mm

------------------------------------------------------------

Director #17 Position : 690 mm , Length : 51 mm

Distance Dir. #16 - Dir. #17 : 49 mm

------------------------------------------------------------

Director #18 Position : 739 mm , Length : 51 mm

Distance Dir. #17 - Dir. #18 : 49 mm

------------------------------------------------------------

Directors / Parasitics are isolated.

Please     choose     an     isolater     thicker     than     :     3     mm

# Appendix III: A Helical Antenna Calculator

Changpuak also keeps a very nice helical antenna calculator on the website. See the URL:

https://www.changpuak.ch/electronics/calc_12a.php

For our purposes, remember that most wifi is linearly polarized. However, reflected signals (from buildings, vehicles, terrain, aircraft, etc) may arrive at any angle. I have found signals from circularly polarized antennas to be more stable when there is a lot of multipath.

This may be useful to you in building a feed for a parabolic dish, suitable for any of the newer Wifi bands or 5G mobile data service. Many techies would simply mount a dongle at the focus, but a top notch system could use a well made helical antenna → short cable → wireless device.

Here is an example of a helical calculation for 5 GHz Wifi:

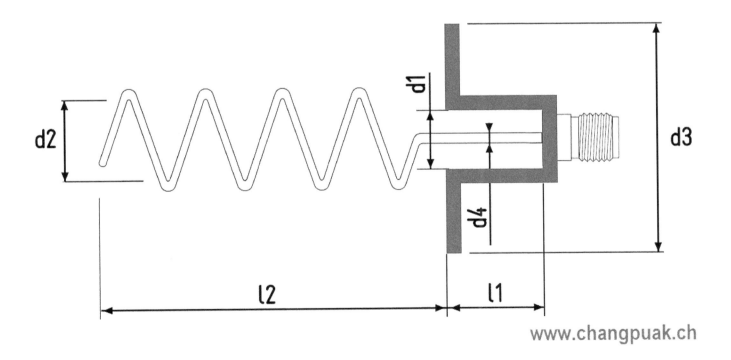

www.changpuak.ch

Ajarn Changpuak Helical Antenna Calculator (cont'd)


Frequency:    5950 MHz

Turns n:        10

λ:                  50.21 mm     (wavelength)

Gain:         15.78 dB

| l1: | 12.55 mm | Length of matching Coax (λ/4) |
|-----|----------|-------------------------------|
| d1: | 6.06 mm | Diameter of matching Coax |
| d4: | 1.50 mm | Wire diameter |
| l2: | 125.52 mm | Length of Helix |
| d2: | 15.98 mm | Helix Diameter |
| d3: | 55.23 mm | Disc Diameter |


Dimensions associated with these wavelengths are small, where less than a tenth of a millimeter makes a difference. Performance will not be good at all if construction is not to very tight tolerances; I would suggest having the antenna constructed in a machine shop unless you have the necessary tools and skills.

Be that as it may, there are people in the amateur radio service who construct antennas and feedhorns for far shorter wavelengths. Again, the key is ability to measure, cut, grind, solder, and polish materials to tolerances                    well                    below                    one                    millimeter.

# ABOUT THE AUTHOR

Philip G. Collier has been a radio enthusiast since the mid 1970s and enjoys writing about radio, travel, and piloting the heavy jets. He is enthusiastic about free and open source software and has published customized versions of the Linux operating system. A webmaster since 2006, Collier has been running websites which help people improve their lives using radio and computing technology. Visit AB9IL.net, SkywaveLinux.com, CatbirdLinux.com, and MOFOLinux.com to discover more of his works.